Endorsements for *Fa*

"Sharing delightful memories from her ~~p~~
storyteller style to weave principles fro
with fresh insights into the lives of eight biblical women. Each chapter
unveils a nugget of truth that challenges women to maintain unhindered faith. I know you will enjoy this new Bible study as much
as I have."

—**Jeannie Vogel** is the author of four Bible studies, including her
most recent one, *Engage: Influencing Your World like Jesus.* Jeannie
has a master's degree in biblical studies and serves as a pastor's
wife, mom, Bible teacher, and women's ministry consultant for
the Northeast Fellowship of Independent Baptist Churches.

"Debbie draws us to herself, endearing us to her family, especially her
grandma, even taking us to the family farm. Instinctively we relate
and want to know her better, and before we know it, Deb also draws
us to women in Scripture whose faith we also want to know better. In
so doing, she provides a reality check for our own faith. Using short
answer questions, she helps us put ourselves in each woman's sandals,
gently pushing us toward unhindered faith."

—**Pat Warren** is the author of the women's Bible study *Weighed by
the Word.* She also co-authored two Bible studies with her husband,
David, and served as his assistant when he was state representative of the Ohio Association of Regular Baptist Churches. With
an MA from Wright State University, Pat taught as an adjunct
English instructor at Cedarville University.

FAITH
unhindered

FAITH
unhindered

FINDING
THE FREEDOM
TO TRUST GOD
COMPLETELY

DEBBIE ASHLEY

REDEMPTION
PRESS

Published by Redemption Press, PO Box 427, Enumclaw, WA 98022.
Toll-Free (844) 2REDEEM (273-3336)

Redemption Press is honored to present this title in partnership with the author. The views expressed or implied in this work are those of the author. Redemption Press provides our imprint seal representing design excellence, creative content, and high-quality production.

The author has tried to recreate events, locales, and conversations from memories of them. In order to maintain their anonymity, in some instances the names of individuals, some identifying characteristics, and some details may have been changed, such as physical properties, occupations, and places of residence.

ISBN 13: 978-1-64645-439-6 (Paperback)
978-1-64645-440-2 (ePub)
978-1-64645-438-9 (Mobi)

Library of Congress Catalog Card Number: 2021917776

Dedication

To Mark, my husband of thirty-five years: Whether it has been nurturing our three children into adulthood, standing by each other through the highs and lows of full-time pastoral ministry, or picking up the slack when one of us is knee deep in a project (your doctoral thesis, my first book project), I would not have wanted to do any of it without you. I dedicate this book to you. Thank you for always believing in me!

Faith in God works—
it just doesn't work
for me.

—Debbie Ashley

Contents

Acknowledgments 11

Introduction: *The Family Farm* 13

Part 1: Finding a Faith That Works—*The Old Pump* 15

   Chapter 1: Letting Go of Disappointment (*Hannah*) . . 19

   Chapter 2: Letting Go of Distractions (*Martha*) 27

Part 2: Discovering God Is Already There—*The Best Doughnuts* 35

   Chapter 3: Letting Go of the Past (*The Samaritan Woman*) 39

   Chapter 4: Letting Go of Fear (*Esther*) 47

Part 3: Seeking God's Treasure in the Rubble—*The Fire* . . . 55

   Chapter 5: Letting Go of What I Love (*Lot's Wife*) . . . 59

   Chapter 6: Letting Go of Rejection (*Hagar*) 67

Part 4: Giving God Access to My Tough Stuff—*The Back Room* 75

   Chapter 7: Letting Go of Criticism (*Miriam*) 79

   Chapter 8: Letting Go of Bitterness (*Job's Wife*) 87

Acknowledgments

Thank you to the team at Redemption Press for the instruction, insights, and encouragement you have provided me throughout the process of bringing this book into print. Your support has been invaluable!

To my church family, with whom I have had the privilege of living, loving, and serving for the past thirty years alongside my husband/pastor: As we have shared our journeys together, you have challenged and inspired me to learn more about God and desire to be more like Christ. This book comes from a grateful heart for all you have taught me.

To my prayer team for this book, Pam, Kathy, Tonya, Ronnie, Penny, Connie: Knowing you were always available to pray for me on this writing journey was immeasurably valuable. Whether in response to a quick text or a long email, your prayers held me up and kept me focused on the God we love and serve. Thank you!

To Mom, Dad, and Julie: Thank you for modeling for me what it means to love God and serve others. Thank you also for instilling in me an unwavering love for family. The lessons I have learned from you and those in our family who have gone before us remain with me and prompted the ideas for this book.

To my children, Jon, Joel and Jenna, and my daughters-in-law, Kelly and Amy: You are each an inspiration to me in your own way, whether it is in your determination to reach a goal, try a new idea, or make a difference in the places where God has placed you. I am grateful for your constant support whenever I have pursued a new challenge, including this writing project.

The Family Farm

I ALWAYS LEANED FORWARD IN MY SEAT WHENEVER OUR FAMILY CAR drove over the little hill on the road to my grandparents' place and their stately white farmhouse came into view. A long-handled red pump stood sentry over an old well, and there we would turn onto the long drive. The milk house greeted us on the left, and the corn crib offered its salutation on the right. A barn filled with cows came next, followed by an old garage that held Grandpa's Ford Model A. The dogs barked their hellos when they heard our tires crunch the gravel. Soon we were slipping off our boots in the mudroom and running up the short stairway to the farmhouse kitchen where Grandma was waiting. The oven's warmth echoed the coziness of Grandma's embrace as she welcomed us.

Sometimes I wish I could go back to the farm for just one day. One day of experiencing the freedom of a little girl running out to play without a care in the world. One day of embracing the unique rhythms of farm life and the pleasure of being with people I loved. One day to remember what it was like when dreams were large and problems were small.

In the summer of 2003, my dream of an ideal life changed suddenly. While on an extended family vacation in California, my oldest son began experiencing symptoms of a severe illness. Upon arriving back home, I made a doctor's appointment. Weight loss and fatigue had overtaken him. I was dreading the diagnosis I expected to hear. The blood work the doctor ordered quickly confirmed my worst fear: my son had juvenile diabetes.

I had wanted so much to hear something else! Something that could be treated with an antibiotic. Something that would go away. But instead, my son, who had been a healthy, active teenager just weeks before, now had a disease he would have to manage every single day.

To say that his life—our lives—changed at that moment is an understatement. Like a stranger who moves in unannounced and decides to stay, diabetes made everything familiar feel uncomfortable. As his mom, I feared making a mistake with his medicine or diet and triggering serious consequences. Even a simple trip away from home, whether for a few hours or a few days, necessitated a higher level of preparation than before. While I knew I needed to be strong and confident for my son and family, inside my heart was breaking. Where was God when this happened? He could have prevented this disease. Why didn't he stop it?

What circumstances have you encountered that you never wanted to face? A dreaded diagnosis from a doctor? The word "divorce" from the man you expected to be married to forever? Hateful words from a rebellious child? Betrayal by someone you trusted? Perhaps you see others seemingly trouble free and wonder why you can't have that. Experiences of rejection, disappointment, distraction, or loss have brought your faith to a standstill.

My friend, if you long for a belief in God that is unhindered by the what-ifs and why-nots, you are not alone. I invite you to join me on this journey to a faith unhindered as we consider women of the past who faced hard circumstances. Discover with me how God can use even the most tragic situations to show us he is there and he is trustworthy.

PART 1

Finding a Faith That Works

The Old Pump

THE LONG-HANDLED RED PUMP HAD MAINTAINED ITS STATELY STANCE AT the entrance to the farmhouse driveway for many years. Large stone slabs covered the main access to the deep well, protecting against any dangerous falls into the cavern below. The earliest residents of the farmhouse had relied on the well's fresh water. With just a few swift pumps on the long handle—up, down, up, down—clear, cold water burst forth and filled their buckets.

But some time ago, water lines were buried along the road in front of the farmhouse, and the farmhouse occupants no longer needed the well. Its water supply slowly diminished until the pump could only rarely draw water from its depths. Still, the worn pump stood tall at the end of the driveway, a reminder of its years of usefulness.

Occasionally, after a hard rain, higher groundwater levels in the well allowed the old pump to work again. My sister and I would ask Grandma for an old jar or bucket. We then took turns lifting and lowering the pump handle. Even though our arms began to tire, we kept going, waiting to hear the distinct gurgling sound of water traveling up the invisible pipe from the cavern below and out the rusty spigot. Most of the time, we had little success with that old pump. But whenever cool, clear water began to trickle into our bucket, we cheered. The pump still worked!

Sometimes our faith can feel like that old pump. We remember past days when we felt confident in God's plan for us. Days when we exercised our faith and saw God answer our prayers. Days when our faith worked.

But when we lose confidence in God's plan and our prayers seem to no longer work, we question the usefulness of our faith. Our spiritual well runs dry. Sure, we may have fleeting experiences of faith, like the occasional trickling water that old pump produced. But those bursts of belief fade quickly. Without regular exercise, our faith grows weak. So we tire of waiting. We give up. We believe faith in God still works—it just doesn't work for me.

We can fill our spiritual well with faith again as we remove the disappointments and distractions that stand in the way and reconnect our belief systems to God's enduring resources.

Faith unhindered becomes a reality when I recognize the hindrances that prevent me from believing God.

CHAPTER 1

Letting Go of Disappointment

SOMEONE'S WORDS LONG AGO CUT THROUGH YOU LIKE A KNIFE, AND you still remember them as if it happened yesterday. An old misunderstanding can never be made right, and it haunts you. The dream you never realized despite your best efforts still weighs you down. Like the old pump, you have worked hard, you have waited, you have wished for more. But trying rarely seems worth doing anymore. Nothing ever turns out right.

Navigating Life's Hurts

As Hannah carried the basket of produce into their house in the hill country of Ephraim, she heard the pitter-patter of little feet crossing the courtyard again. It seemed there was always a little one underfoot. And always a hungry mouth to feed.

If only she could say one of them belonged to her. But that had not been her lot in life. Despite a supportive husband, Elkanah, Hannah's empty heart reflected her empty womb, and nothing seemed able to fill the void.

It's not as though she hadn't prayed about it. Of course she had. She knew God was the source of life and the giver of all good gifts from above. She believed he had a plan for her and would fulfill it in his good time and way. She desired to please him and sensed his pleasure in her.

But still, she had no child.

Hannah turned her attention back to the basket of produce on the table. Ah, yes, the trip! They were preparing to travel, and she needed to have the food provisions ready for all those in their group. She packed bread and honey in the basket and then silently counted the figs: one for her, one for her husband, one for her husband's other wife, two for the other wife's children . . .

Heartache swelled up inside her again, threatening to drown her spirit. She tried hard to control it, but it always caught her by surprise, taking her breath away as the weight of her pain overcame her. *God, when will this hurt ever end?*

Hannah wondered how she had gotten into this situation. The marriage between her and Elkanah had started so happy. She had felt confident in God's plan for them. But then came the troubling years of no pregnancy. For a while, Hannah allowed herself to get her hopes up. But she eventually grew tired of the disappointment.

Then came the day—that one devastating day—with the turn of events she never saw coming. A new wife! How could he do that to her? Just because it was an acceptable custom didn't mean it was God's plan for them! Deep rivers of hurt cut through Hannah's soul when Peninnah moved in. And when Peninnah's new baby came into the family less than a year later, Hannah's pain grew almost unbearable.

Elkanah tried to understand Hannah. But he asked her why she was so consumed with having a child. Wasn't he enough? Didn't he take care of her and even bless her with more than her share of his wealth? Why couldn't she let go of her dream of being a mother and just be content?

And then there was Peninnah. The birth of her first child had created trouble enough, but when other children followed, the gloating began, and the place of disgrace became Hannah's permanent role.

Tired of rehearsing the painful sequence of past events, Hannah turned her attention back to preparations for the trip. These days when they all traveled to the temple together were the hardest days of each year. She had nowhere to go to get away from it all. But she went willingly, both to support her husband and to please God.

When they arrived in Shiloh this time, Hannah found the situation particularly difficult. Everyone had something to do except her.

Elkanah, oblivious to her heartache over her unanswered prayers, busied himself with activities at the temple. And Peninnah, attending to the children, seemed particularly bent on making fun of her.

Finally, Hannah could take it no longer. She stood near the front entrance of the temple as if to separate herself from the rest of the family. Heart-wrenching sobs shook her body. Not speaking a word, just moving her lips, Hannah cried out to God, begging him to give her a child. And with a passion coming from deep within her soul, she vowed to God that if he gave her a son, she would give him back to God to serve him in the temple all the days of his life.

As the last whisper left her lips, Hannah realized everyone was watching her, including the priest, whose furrowed brow revealed his displeasure with her. As if her current humiliation was not enough, he called her out in front of everyone for being drunk. How was it that everyone misunderstood her? Her husband, Peninnah, even the priest! Did God understand her?

A year later, the gentle cries of a newborn were heard in Elkanah and Hannah's house. Soon the pitter-patter of her own son's feet greeted her ears as she put away produce from the market. And three years later, Hannah took her young son, Samuel, to the temple, where she dedicated him to God's service. God had indeed answered her prayers and filled her heart with joy. Now she demonstrated her great love for God by keeping the promise she had made to him.

Unhindered faith believes in God's ability to answer my prayer and trusts God to take care of the situations and people that matter the most to me.

Deepening Our Understanding

What has been your greatest disappointment recently? Or what has been your greatest disappointment ever? How have you coped with this disappointment?

_____

_____

_____

_____

_____

_____

When Circumstances Cause Disappointment *(Read 1 Samuel 1:1–2)*

The first few verses of this chapter introduce the three primary characters of the story. Elkanah is a faithful worshiper of God and takes his family to the temple in Shiloh every year. He is also the husband of two wives, Hannah and Peninnah. The passage identifies a distinct difference between these two women: Peninnah has children, but Hannah has none.

In the culture and time in which Hannah lives, it is considered shameful for a woman to be barren. A closed womb indicates a lack of God's blessing. Imagine Hannah's disappointment at being unable to give birth to a child. Then consider the weight of the shame she also carries because of her barrenness. The grief Hannah feels over her circumstances must run deep.

1. Hannah has reason to be disappointed with her difficult circumstances. What emotions do you think she feels? How might her situation have affected her view of God?

_____

_____

_____

_____

_____

2. What circumstances have caused you to feel disappointed with your life? How has this disappointment affected you? How has it affected your view of God?

_____

_____

_____

_____

_____

When People Cause Disappointment *(Read 1 Samuel 1:3–16)*
Elkanah knows of Hannah's sorrow over her inability to have children. Yet he seems unaware of how best to meet her unique needs, wishing instead that she could let go of her desire for a child and be content with him. And Peninnah, the other wife, makes no attempt to encourage or comfort Hannah. Instead, she provokes Hannah continuously, to the point of causing her great pain.

The stress in the family relationships goes on year after year, especially when they travel to the temple. While there, Hannah weeps often and eats rarely. Even the priest, Eli, misunderstands her. He observes the regular flow of Jewish worshipers in and out of the temple—those who arrive with great joy to worship God and those who arrive with heavy hearts to plead with him. But when Hannah stands up, alone, just outside the temple, silently pleading with God for a child, Eli accuses her of being drunk.

3. Hannah has reason to be disappointed with the significant people in her life. What are the specific emotions she might have experienced because of the failure of others to understand her?

_____

_____

_____

_____

_____

4. In what way has someone in the past or present significantly disappointed you? How has this occurrence affected you?

_____

_____

_____

_____

_____

When God Steps In _(Read 1 Samuel 1:17–2:11)_

After Hannah explains to Eli that she is not drunk but fervently praying to God for a child, Eli speaks words of blessing over her. Hannah leaves the temple with renewed hope. A year later, she has become the mother of a young son named Samuel. She returns to the temple three years later to dedicate her son to a lifetime in God's service. While at the temple, Hannah expresses another prayer to God—this time a prayer of praise and rejoicing.

5. What characteristics of God does Hannah mention in her prayer? How might she have learned this about God through the disappointments she had previously experienced?

_____

_____

_____

_____

_____

6. Consider the disappointments you have faced. Has God ever stepped in and changed your disappointment to joy? If so, what did you learn about him through this experience?

_____

_____

_____

_____

_____

Journal Response

You may find yourself in circumstances where, like Hannah, you aren't exactly angry with God, but you are disappointed with him. What is God allowing right now that doesn't make sense to you?

_____

_____

_____

_____

_____

_____

Prayer Response

The turning point in Hannah's story of disappointment is her prayer at the temple. What disappointments hinder your faith in God? Are you willing to express your disappointment to him in prayer? Will you give your disappointments to him, trusting him for the outcome?

_____

_____

_____

_____

_____

_____

> _I encourage you to run to him when you are beaten down, broken into pieces, questioning your faith, and doubting his goodness. If you listen, you will hear him say ... "There is nothing that will ever take away my unconditional love for you." Get used to it. God loves people who don't have all the answers._
>
> —Carol Kent[1]

---

1. Carol Kent, _When I Lay My Isaac Down_ (Colorado Springs, CO: NavPress, 2004), 186.

CHAPTER 2

Letting Go of Distractions

B<small>ILLS</small>, <small>TEXTS</small>, <small>LAUNDRY</small>, <small>GROCERIES</small>, <small>BASEBALL PRACTICE</small>, <small>MOWING THE</small> lawn, caring for an elderly parent—you're trying to keep it all together, but your head is spinning. You can't think straight, let alone concentrate on the important stuff. When will the whirlwind slow down?

Finding a New Focus

Martha banged the iron kettle on the table a little harder this time, hoping someone would notice. But it didn't work. It seemed she was the only person in the house who understood what it took to get all the work done around here. It was bad enough trying to keep up on a normal day, with family members coming and going. But today was worse. Guests were coming over for dinner, and apparently, everyone had conveniently disappeared from the kitchen.

Martha slid her knife swiftly through the vegetables as her mind flew through a list of all the times her family had left her to do the work alone. Today the culprit was her sister. Mary seemed blissfully unaware of all the preparations still needed before dinner. In fact, where was she?

Voices in the sunlit courtyard signaled to Martha that the guests were settling in and enjoying jovial conversation with one another. Ah, yes, she could hear Mary's voice, too, chiming in with the crowd. Martha moved faster, stirring the simmering broth in the kettle even as anger simmered inside her spirit. Then, finally able to take a break, she wiped her hands on her apron, brushed the sweat off her forehead, and forced a weak smile as she joined the crowd in the courtyard.

At first no one even noticed her. The people had gathered around the most important guest, Jesus. And there was her sister, Mary, sitting at the very front near Jesus's feet, listening to every word he said.

Martha tried to get Mary's attention, but her sister never looked her way. So Martha walked through the crowd, stepping around people until she stood in front of Jesus, next to Mary, who looked up in surprise. The conversations in the room trickled to nothing but stark silence.

Martha blurted, "Jesus, don't you care about me? Can't you see my sister isn't helping me?" She didn't wait for an answer. "Tell her to help me!" Tears fell down her cheeks as she caught her breath, trying not to sob. But before she could turn away, Jesus spoke her name—twice. Not in anger but with compassion, as he always did. He had seen her agitation, but unlike her, he knew the reason for it—the agitation wasn't her sister's fault. It was her own.

As always, Jesus saw through to her soul. He recognized her anxiety. He had compassion for her troubled spirit. And as always, he showed her a way out—a way to set aside the distractions that had caused her anxiety, a way to embrace the one thing he knew she needed. Just one thing. The one thing her sister had already chosen—to be with Jesus.

Unhindered faith grows when I recognize and remove the distractions that prevent me from spending time with Jesus.

Deepening Our Understanding

What is on your to-do list for today? Write some of these items below.
Will you be able to accomplish everything on your list?

———————————————————————————

———————————————————————————

———————————————————————————

———————————————————————————

———————————————————————————

Recognize the Surprise of Distraction *(Read Luke 10:38–39a)*

As Jesus passes through the town of Bethany, Martha invites him to
stay for dinner in her family's home, which he visited often. Martha
begins dinner preparations, but the process doesn't go as planned. She
has counted on the help of her sister, but Mary leaves the kitchen.
Perhaps Martha has tried to do too many things in the time she has.
It's easy to make this mistake, isn't it?

Sometimes we have the best-laid plans for how to accomplish
everything on our to-do list, but the day just doesn't go that way. Or
life just doesn't go that way. We are caught by surprise, and the very
thing we expect to enjoy becomes a distraction that derails us.

1. Do you think Martha enjoyed hospitality? Do you think
   Martha's attitude was different when Jesus was the guest?

———————————————————————————

———————————————————————————

———————————————————————————

———————————————————————————

2. How do you feel about having people in your home for a
   meal or social event? How would you feel if the guest coming
   to your home was Jesus?

———————————————————————————

———————————————————————————

———————————————————————————

———————————————————————————

Remember the True Source of Distraction (*Read Luke 10:39b–40*)

As Jesus settles into Mary and Martha's home, he uses the time before the meal to teach. The story gives no indication of how many people are in the home at this time. Perhaps it is just family. Maybe a few others have come in along with Jesus. No one else is named. Mary is the one in focus as she sits at the feet of Jesus, taking in every word he says.

Martha levels her complaint against her sister, who is obviously not helping her with meal preparations. But Martha indirectly communicates her disappointment with Jesus as well. In reality, neither Mary nor Jesus is the true source of Martha's distraction.

3. What does Martha suggest about Jesus's attitude toward her in the question she asks him? Who does Martha hold indirectly responsible for her distraction and agitation?

_____

_____

_____

_____

_____

4. What person or persons are most often the targets of your agitation? What do they typically do—or fail to do—that bothers you? Are they truly responsible for your distraction and agitation?

_____

_____

_____

_____

_____

Realize the Problem of Distraction (*Read Luke 10:41*)

Jesus points out the reason for Martha's distraction, referring to the many things Martha is doing, though he does not list specifics. This remark contrasts with Jesus's next comment, in which he describes the one thing Mary has chosen—a choice that has freed her from distraction and agitation.

5.   What two words does Jesus use to describe Martha's state of mind?

_____

_____

_____

_____

_____

6.   What words might Jesus use to describe your state of mind right now? Or how might a friend or family member describe your state of mind?

_____

_____

_____

_____

_____

Regain a Right Perspective on Distraction *(Read Luke 10:42)*
Jesus mentions to Martha the one thing Mary has chosen, calling it "the good portion." Jesus does not criticize Martha for working in the kitchen instead of sitting at his feet next to Mary. He knows the necessity of preparing and serving a meal, no doubt also grateful for her hospitality. Yet Jesus recognizes that Martha has lost perspective, failing to see the value in both worship and work.

7.   What is the "good thing" that Mary has done? What phrase does Jesus use to describe the difference between what Mary and Martha have chosen?

_____

_____

_____

_____

8. Responsibilities are a part of daily life. Distractions are inevitable. Finding a balance between our work and our worship is a challenge. How can choosing *the good thing that will not be taken away* help us manage distractions?

_____

_____

_____

_____

Remember How Much Jesus Loves You *(Read John 11:1–5)*
None of us wants to be remembered for one bad day we had. The Bible reveals that Jesus spends time with Martha on other occasions, particularly when Mary and Martha are dealing with the serious illness of their brother Lazarus. We are told in these verses that Jesus loves Martha. He does not have favorites. He does not love Mary better. In fact, when Jesus comes to their home, Martha steps out to meet him first while Mary remains in the house (John 11:20).

9. When someone is dying, our first instinct is to call the people we feel closest to. When Martha's brother is dying, her first instinct is to call Jesus. What does this tell you about Martha's relationship with Jesus, even after the previous incident of her complaint against her sister?

_____

_____

_____

_____

10. Has there been a time when you felt as though you ruined your relationship with God and he was not happy with you anymore? Would you like to restore that relationship?

_____

_____

_____

_____

Renew Your Commitment to Serve with an Undistracted Heart *(Read John 12:1–8)*

At another time, Jesus comes to the house of Mary, Martha, and Lazarus, where they host a dinner in Jesus's honor. Martha is serving again. Lazarus reclines at the table near Jesus. Mary, in an act of worship, anoints Jesus's feet with expensive perfume. No mention is made of Martha feeling stressed or upset with her role in this event. Each of them expresses their love for Jesus in a different way, sometimes as a worker and sometimes as a worshipper. But they are all intent on spending time with Jesus.

11. Is it possible to express our love for Jesus in diverse ways? Sometimes serving? Sometimes sitting at his feet? What would enable you to do both with an undistracted heart?

_____

_____

_____

_____

_____

Journal Response

Distractions are an inevitable part of every day. Our minds are cluttered with decisions, problems, responsibilities, hopes, and sorrows. What are practical ways you might remove the hindrance of distractions, allowing you to spend more time with Jesus?

_____

_____

_____

_____

_____

_____

Prayer Response

Just like Martha, it is important to remember that Jesus loves you, to remember what God has done for you, and to remember to be both a worshipper and a worker. Write a simple prayer to God, expressing your thoughts to him about what these truths mean to you.

_____

_____

_____

_____

_____

_____

At the end of the day, Jesus doesn't count how many guests you had over for dinner, how many diapers you changed, or how many emails you answered at the office. It's not that these things don't matter to him. It's just that these things don't last. What Mary chose, and what we need to choose over all the other business of life, is the one thing that will never be taken away from us—the time we spend with Jesus.

—Debbie Ashley

PART 2

Discovering God Is
Already There

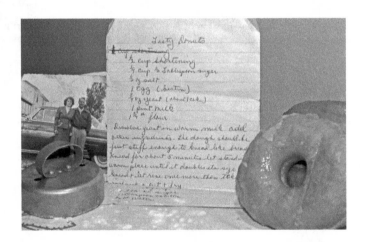

The Best Doughnuts

EVERY YEAR DURING OUR SPRING BREAK FROM SCHOOL, MY MOM, SISTER, and I would spend a day at the farm with Grandma, making the best homemade doughnuts ever. By the time we arrived, Grandma was already in the kitchen hard at work. She woke extra early those mornings to complete her farm chores, feeding the barn cats and checking on the cows. Then, returning to the kitchen, she would put on her well-worn kitchen apron and mix and knead the dough.

Dropping our coats by the door and stepping into the cheery kitchen, we could see the dough had already risen well above the rim of the round metal pot she always used for this purpose. Grandma would let my sister and me punch down the huge blob of dough with our fists, listening to the popping sounds as the yeasty air bubbles deflated. We always arrived just in time for the fun to start!

Now that the dough was ready, Grandma covered her farm-house table with a colorful plastic tablecloth and then gave each of us a portion of dough to roll out. Its tangy yet sweet scent made my mouth water as I flattened it with a rolling pin. Then Grandma handed my sister and me her metal doughnut cutters. We excitedly pressed them into the soft dough, pulling out both doughnuts and tiny doughnut holes.

Next, Grandma gently dropped the formed rounds of dough into the kettle of oil she had heated. They sizzled until they were crispy brown on both sides. Using a long-handled fork, she carefully lifted each doughnut out of the oil, placing it on a tray to drain.

Then came the fun part—dipping them in the thin sugar glaze. If the fried pastries were too hot, the glaze would simply run off. If they were too cool, the glaze became sticky. Grandma knew how to do it exactly right. We could hardly wait to bite into those fresh-glazed treats. When all the doughnuts had been fried and glazed, we packaged them into boxes so that a dozen or so could be delivered to each of her six grandchildren.

I realize now that making doughnuts with Grandma was so much fun because she had been hard at work in the kitchen before we arrived, making sure everything was ready for us. When I have tried to make her doughnuts, I understand how much work she had to do for us. And I appreciate her even more.

Faith unhindered begins with understanding that God has already done the work for me.

CHAPTER 3

Letting Go of the Past

YOU HAVE WORKED HARD TO GET WHERE YOU ARE IN LIFE. YOU HAVE fought for every ounce of respect and pushed through every wave of criticism. You have put the past in its place and pressed forward for a better future. Yet, in spite of all these efforts, you still feel as though you are losing. It is at these moments you realize you can't fix the problems that matter on your own. You need someone to step in and help.

Seeking Living Water

A subtle smile slipped across the woman's lips as she made her way through the dusty streets of Sychar, Samaria. The morning sun was bright, but its heat had not yet fully taken hold of the day. Walking past neighbors already washing their linens after fetching water from the well, she caught snippets of the gossip they tossed out to one another. Most of it she already knew but found interesting nonetheless. At least the town talk was no longer about her. They had grown tired of clucking their tongues about her situation and just left her alone, which suited her perfectly.

Turning the corner on the path out of town, the woman made her way to the local well. Expecting to see no one, the sight of a weary stranger sitting there pulled her up short. Her brows furrowed a bit as she recognized the Jewish design of his robe. What was a Jewish man doing here? She wasn't sure how to approach the well. Could she, a Samaritan—and a woman at that—approach this Jew and get him to move out of her way so she could draw her water? It wasn't done! Someone would have yet another bit of juicy gossip to tell about her if she did. But the Jewish stranger's words interrupted her thoughts.

"Will you give me a drink of water?" he asked, his voice dry with thirst.

She slowly placed her bucket on the ground. Was this a trick? Surely, he could see she was a Samaritan and a woman. "Why are you talking to me?" As soon as the question escaped her lips, she wished she hadn't asked. But it was too late.

His gentle answer puzzled her. "You don't know who I am."

Her stomach churned. *You don't know who I am either.*

The stranger told her of living water, water that could eliminate thirst forever.

Intrigued, she asked another question. "So are you greater than Jacob, our nation's great forefather who provided this well for us?"

He didn't seem to hear her question. Instead, he continued talking about this living water. And something about eternal life.

She was unsure what this stranger meant by eternal life, but she did know that eliminating her daily trips to this well would be helpful. "Sir, give me this water." She wasn't sure exactly what she had expected, but nothing could have prepared her for his next comment.

"Go call your husband," he instructed her.

Why did he have to ask about a husband? Had someone in town already gotten to this man and told him all about her? Did he know she was living with a man who was not her husband? Not ready to reveal the truth, she replied, "I don't have a husband."

The stranger nodded in agreement. "You are right," he said. "You don't have a husband now, but you have had five previous husbands."

Now her mind was racing. This was no ordinary traveler stopping by on his way through town. This must be a man of God, a prophet—someone who could see inside people, inside her own heart. She recalled teachings she had heard before. Talk of a Messiah to come. One who would tell them all things. One who would lead them to worship God from the heart, in spirit and in truth. Could this be the Messiah, the one they had been waiting for?

As if reading her mind, the Jewish stranger answered her questioning spirit with these simple words, "I who speak to you am he."

Joy arose in her so suddenly that the squint of her eyes no longer came from the burning sun but from her unhindered smile. This man had to be the Messiah, the Savior of the world. And he offered her forgiveness and acceptance! She didn't have to work to earn a place in God's presence. A freedom she had never known before swept over her. For the first time, she was completely known and understood by someone—and his name was Jesus. And all those neighbors and townsfolk from whom she had stayed distant looked different to her now. She didn't have to hide anymore. She had to tell them the Messiah was here! How could she keep this good news to herself? If Jesus knew everything about her and still loved her, he could do the same for them.

Unhindered faith begins when I open my heart to Jesus by accepting his love and forgiveness of my sins, paid for by his death on the cross.

Deepening Our Understanding

Have you ever experienced an awkward conversation with someone you barely knew? Maybe a job interview with a potential employer did not go well. Or you may have had an unfriendly discussion with a neighbor who was unhappy with you. Describe your feelings during and after this awkward situation:

_____

_____

_____

_____

_____

_____

Jesus Expresses His Need *(Read John 4:1–9)*

The Samaritan woman's contact with Jesus begins with an awkward conversation between two individuals who would never expect to talk to each other in this setting. In this time, women do not enjoy the same rights and freedoms as men, and Samaritans and Jews do not mix. Despite the cultural barriers, Jesus starts a conversation with her, knowing that, under the circumstances, she would never initiate a conversation with him. He begins by asking her a question expressing a common human need: "Will you give me a drink?" Jesus reaches out to her across the human barriers that should separate them and draws her into the conversation with a need common to every living being—a need so personal, so essential to life, that it is impossible to ignore.

1. What barriers exist that make the woman's conversation with Jesus feel uncomfortable? How do you think these cultural realities might affect her view of herself and her situation?

_____

_____

_____

_____

_____

2. Are you aware of any barriers of your own that stand in the way of a personal relationship with Jesus? If so, what are these barriers and how might they be a hindrance?

_____

_____

_____

_____

_____

_____

Jesus Recognizes Her Need *(Read John 4:10–15)*

Using the analogy of water, Jesus turns the woman's attention away from his physical need to her spiritual need. While they began the conversation talking about the literal water she came to draw from the well, Jesus tells her of a living water that will do far more than meet a physical need. This living water will satisfy a spiritual need common to every person: the need for eternal life.

3. Looking at the woman's response to Jesus (v. 15), what need is she still focused on?

_____

_____

_____

_____

_____

_____

4. Which of your own needs currently occupy your thoughts most often?

_____

_____

_____

_____

_____

_____

Jesus Clarifies Her Need *(Read John 4:16–19)*

Turning the attention away from the water, Jesus tells the woman to do something specific—bring her husband to the well. Perhaps a little startled by this shift in the conversation, she replies with a simple explanation that she does not have a husband.

True.

But Jesus does not let her leave the subject there. He gently reveals to her that he knows her personal history in detail. He does not do this to criticize or trap her. He makes no disapproving comments on her life choices. Instead, he uses this moment of truth to make known to her that he is not a man with normal limitations of knowledge and power. Yet he has chosen to spend this time in intimate conversation with her.

5. What might be the woman's internal response when she realizes Jesus knows all about her past and present situations?

_____

_____

_____

_____

_____

6. Jesus knows all about you too—your past and your present. How does that fact make you feel? Circle any that apply:

Relieved   A little nervous   Indifferent   Happy   Uncomfortable

Jesus Meets Her Need *(Read John 4:20–30, 39–42)*

As the Samaritan woman discerns she is speaking with a prophet, she shifts the conversation to religious questions, particularly about worship. Jesus explains that a time is coming when the worship of God will no longer be defined by a physical location but will take place in the heart. And then, in perhaps the most astounding revelation of this conversation, Jesus tells the woman that he, the Messiah, is standing before her, answering her questions and offering to meet her need for eternal life. She does not have to live with rejection any longer. He accepts her. She does not have to bear the burden of her sin and guilt. He forgives her. All the barriers have been removed. A new freedom is hers, found in her faith in Jesus.

7. How would you describe your relationship with Jesus at this time? What, if any, hindrances stand in your way? How might the lessons of this story help you find the same freedom the woman of Samaria finds in Jesus?

_____

_____

_____

_____

_____

After the Samaritan woman realizes who Jesus is, she invites her neighbors to come to the well and meet him. They invite Jesus to stay with them for a few days, which he does. Many of the people from Sychar believe in Jesus, not just from the woman's testimony but from what they learn from Jesus's own words.

8. Was there a time when someone talked with you about Jesus? If so, what did they share with you? How did you respond?

_____

_____

_____

_____

_____

Journal Response

If understanding how to have a relationship with Jesus is new to you, what questions do you have about it? What, if any, hindrances keep you from taking this next step? If you already have a relationship with Jesus, what hindrances are affecting your relationship with him now? What steps do you need to take to deal with these hindrances?

_____
_____
_____
_____
_____
_____

Prayer Response

Perhaps you have a desire to begin a relationship with Jesus by placing your faith in him just as the Samaritan woman did. In this space, write a few phrases or sentences of prayer to God, expressing your desire to him. Or perhaps you have family or friends who have not yet placed their faith in Jesus. In this space, write a few phrases or sentences of prayer to God for those you know who do not have a relationship with Jesus.

_____
_____
_____
_____
_____

What does the gospel say you have been given right here, right now, so that you can be what you've been called to be and do what you've been called to do? The answer is Christ!

—Paul David Tripp[2]

---

2. Paul David Tripp, *New Morning Mercies* (Wheaton, IL: Crossway, 2014), January 18.

CHAPTER 4

Letting Go of Fear

YOU HAVE BEEN THERE BEFORE: THE UNEXPECTED DIAGNOSIS FROM THE doctor, the shocking end to a relationship you expected would last forever, the career you planned on till retirement. These unpleasant surprises are often followed by an unspoken fear: What if something like that happens again? What if my disease comes back? What if a new relationship ends up in the same disaster? What if my job falls through—again?

Staying Strong in Adversity

Esther's hand shook as she read the scroll her attendant had delivered. Her mind reeled as she tried to absorb the disturbing information her uncle Mordecai had sent to her. Nothing had prepared her for this. The complete annihilation of all Jews? By edict of the king? A weight pressed on her chest, taking her breath away as she sank into the nearest chair.

She considered herself a discerning person. She was the queen! She expected to be aware of animosity and divisive plots brewing within the walls of the palace. But somehow she had missed this. A shiver of fear crept up her spine. What else was she unaware of?

Her heart beat faster as she contemplated Mordecai's request that had accompanied the scroll. He wanted her to go to the king and plead for the salvation of her people, the Jews. But it wasn't as easy as that. Esther sent a reply to Mordecai: I know I am the queen, but in this case, I can't enter the king's presence without being invited. I could lose my life. I'm sorry.

Staring out the window in her private chamber, Esther saw the sunlight shining on the meticulous beauty of the palace gardens below. But she couldn't enjoy it anymore. Any sense of peace had been replaced with panic.

She had felt this panic before. Memories came flooding back. The unbearable sorrow of her parents' tragic deaths. The overwhelming helplessness of being an orphaned child. The shocking horror of being taken from her uncle's home and placed in a palace harem, trapped. What if she never saw her uncle again?

But Mordecai had made sure that never happened. He continued to watch over her from a distance, providing the wisdom and instruction she had come to expect from him. And she was also learning that God had been watching over her, directing her steps even as a child, eventually leading her into this influential position as the queen.

With the edict still sitting on her desk, Esther dropped her head into her hands and sobbed. A gentle knock on the door startled her. "Come in," she said, quickly wiping the tears from her eyes. Her attendant had returned with a reply from Mordecai. Though the enormity of his message gripped her heart, a faint smile crossed her lips. Yes, these were indeed words from her uncle. She recognized the resolve, the determination, the courage she had seen in him since she was a child. And she understood the challenge he was giving her. He had always challenged her to do more than she thought she could. He was doing it again. Only this time he was asking her to risk her life.

Deep in her heart, she already knew the answer. She knew what she had to do. Without hesitation, she sent her final response. She asked her uncle for one thing: fervent prayer. And she promised the one thing she could do: go before the king to save her people. This plan could result in her death. Or it could result in the salvation of the entire Jewish nation. But just as she had seen God direct her steps in the past, she knew she could trust God to direct her steps in the future, whatever that future might hold.

Unhindered faith allows me to face an uncertain future with confidence because I can trust in the certainty of God's plan for me.

Deepening Our Understanding

What was one thing you were afraid of as a child? Spiders? Heights?
Storms? Was there a time when you had to face this fear head-on?
How did that experience affect you?

_____

_____

_____

_____

_____

_____

_____

Esther Learns from Her Past *(Read Esther 2:1–14)*

Esther does not become a strong woman in the moment she faces
her greatest challenge as an adult; she becomes a strong woman by
learning from her challenges as a girl. Esther's childhood is difficult.
She is orphaned as a little girl but cared for by a loving uncle named
Mordecai, who takes her into his home as his own daughter.

Esther's nationality creates another difficulty for her. Babylon has
conquered the Jewish people and taken them into exile before Esther
is born. She grows up as a foreigner in this land, now governed by the
Persians. Hatred and animosity toward the Jews abound, so much so
that Mordecai instructs her to hide her Jewish identity. Esther follows
her uncle's wise advice.

Esther's young-adult years bring even more trouble. As a beau-
tiful young woman, she is taken from her uncle and placed in the
harem of the powerful King Xerxes (Ahasuerus) with no possibility
of leaving. Even though Esther wins the favor of those around her in
the harem, she has no reason to believe anything good can come out
of her captivity in this place.

1. Thinking of Esther's experience as an orphan, an outcast, and a captive in a harem, how do you think these circumstances affect her as a young woman? What fears might she face? What other emotions might she have?

_____

_____

_____

_____

2. How have difficult experiences in your past changed you? What fears have you had to face?

_____

_____

_____

_____

_____

Esther Seeks Wise Resources in the Present (Read Esther 4:1–14)

While living as a captive in the harem of a pagan king, Esther knows there are few people she can trust. But Mordecai, her devoted uncle, makes his presence known every day by walking near the courtyard of the harem, seeking information on Esther's well-being. Remarkably, in God's divine plan, Esther receives the king's favor and is chosen to be his new queen. Even in this powerful role, Esther continues to seek out the wisdom of her uncle to direct her.

When Esther is crowned, Hathach becomes her attendant. Later, when Mordecai learns of the disturbing news of a secret plot to destroy the Jews, he mourns publicly in sackcloth and ashes, along with many other Jews. Hathach acquires the accurate information Esther needs from Mordecai, including the exact amount of money set aside for the destruction of the Jews and a copy of the edict demanding Jewish annihilation. If the decree cannot be reversed, the destruction of the Jewish people is imminent.

3. Esther relies on her uncle to provide an accurate assessment of the situation. What might have happened if Esther had reacted based on her own thoughts and emotions rather than seeking the help of others?

_____

_____

_____

_____

_____

4. Have you been willing to listen to wise and direct counsel, even if it is not what you want to hear? Is there someone you trust to provide wise insights about uncertainties you face? Do you need help finding wise resources to properly make decisions about your future?

_____

_____

_____

_____

_____

Esther Chooses a Brave Response to an Unknown Future
(Read Esther 4:15–17)

Mordecai speaks plainly to Esther about the disastrous consequences if she does not take action against the destructive decree to massacre the Jews. So Esther makes a request of her people, asking them to pray and fast for three days. Then Esther states her brave response in five short words: "If I perish, I perish."

This is not a calloused I-don't-care attitude from Esther. She has contemplated all the options. She knows the rules. She knows the consequences. She knows who she is and what she can do. She recognizes her responsibility. She chooses to take the risk and do what is right. And in God's divine plan, Esther's request of the king leads him to reverse the devastating edict, thus saving the Jewish people from annihilation.

An orphan. An outcast. A captive woman in a king's harem. Esther could become bitter because of these circumstances. But she chooses instead to allow these difficulties to make her strong. Because of her past right decisions, she can make the weightiest decision she has ever made with bravery and confidence in God's sovereign control—even if it costs her life.

5. No doubt Esther feels deep fear over her possible execution when she agrees to enter the king's presence unsummoned. She does not hide her fear. Instead, she asks for three days of prayer and fasting before she approaches the king. Why do you think she chooses this plan?

    _____

    _____

    _____

    _____

    _____

6. How do you handle fear? Are you likely to share your fear with others, or do you tend to hide your fear? Using Esther as an example, what are some steps you can take to manage fear and respond bravely to the uncertainties before you?

    _____

    _____

    _____

    _____

    _____

Journal Response

We do not suddenly become brave at the moment we most need it. We become brave when we choose to face daily challenges with right choices. We become brave when we rely on the wise counsel of others to direct us. We become brave when we choose to trust God for unknown outcomes. What would help you remove the hindrance of fear and develop a faith in God that enables you to be brave in even the worst circumstances?

Prayer Response

Has there been a time when you have seen God work out a seemingly impossible situation? Are you in an impossible situation now and you need him to intervene? Write a prayer to God, either expressing your gratitude for his work on your behalf in the past or asking him to intervene in your present circumstances or your future concerns:

> *I know of no greater simplifier for all of life. Whatever happens*
> *is assigned. . . . Every assignment is measured and controlled*
> *for my eternal good. As I accept the given portion, other*
> *options are cancelled. Decisions become much easier, directions*
> *clearer, and hence my heart becomes inexpressibly quieter.*
> —Elizabeth Elliott[3]

---

3. Elisabeth Elliott, *Keep A Quiet Heart* (Ann Arbor, MI: Servant Publications, 1995), 18.

PART 3

Seeking God's Treasure in the Rubble

The Fire

WHEN I WAS AROUND TEN YEARS OLD, MY GRANDPARENTS' ICONIC FARM-house burned to the ground. I still remember that tragic day. Grandma was at our house when the phone rang. As my mom spoke to the person on the other end of the line, I sensed at once something was terribly wrong. Grandma, my sister, and I all stood in the kitchen, trying to prepare ourselves for whatever difficult news was coming. Slowly, my mom hung up the phone. I can still hear her words in my mind today: "Mom, you need to sit down."

The color drained out of Grandma's face as she slumped to the nearest place to sit on the stairs. My mom told her that her house had caught on fire, and there was nothing left. I watched my grandma's face intently even as I tried to grasp the news myself. Mom continued, saying, "Dad is okay. He's there now. I need to take you there. We need to go now."

We all moved toward the door in silence. With every step, my mind raced and lurched. I wanted to shout, "I don't want to go! I don't want to see this! I want things to be the way they were!" But like everyone else, I said nothing.

We made the thirty-minute drive to the farmhouse without speaking a word. As we drove over the little hill in the road, the stately white farmhouse that had always greeted us was gone. Silent spirals of smoke rose from the massive pile of charred remains where the farmhouse had once stood, a glaring sight of destruction in stark contrast to the clear blue sky behind it. Fire trucks filled the driveway, so we pulled over to the side, got out of the car, and sloshed our way through puddles of water as we approached the house. Grandpa, who had arrived at the scene first, trudged over to stand by his wife. They spoke no words between them. Tears burned my eyes and slipped down my cheeks.

Later, we learned the fire had been caused by an electrical surge that burst through the power lines into the farmhouse, melting circuit breakers and turning the wooden structure into a tinderbox. It took several days for the ashes to cool enough to see if anything of value remained. I still remember helping Grandma sift for days through the ashes as we attempted to find old family photos, recipes, jewelry, Bibles, dishes. While little had survived, we did find some photos and a few other family valuables, many of which we still cherish today. After our search, a bulldozer came and pushed all the ruins into a large pile in a field nearby. Only the charred cavern of the former basement remained. The gaping hole in the ground seemed to echo the gaping hole in our hearts from this terrible loss.

Devastating life experiences can make us feel like this—like we are sifting through the smoldering rubble of what our life once was, trying to find anything left of value. When we face the fact that we have nothing left, we have a choice to make. We can shove our faith away along with the rubble, leaving a gaping hole in our hearts. Or we can hold on to what is most precious to us—our faith in God—and ask him to help us look past the disaster, find the treasures, and rebuild our lives on his promises.

Faith unhindered believes that God can bring me through life's most devastating experiences and teach me how to value what matters most.

CHAPTER 5

Letting Go of What I Love

NOTHING IN LIFE COMES EASY, THEY SAY. YOU GET IT. YOU KNOW HOW
hard you have worked to get where you are now—the sacrifices you
have made for your career, for your family, for yourself. You're even
able to occasionally enjoy the good stuff in life, right? Until one day,
tragedy strikes. And in that moment, you are forced to decide what
really matters most.

Choosing God's Best

Even as a little girl, Lot's wife had loved city life. There was so much to
do and enjoy! She found the allure of Sodom enchanting. And as she
grew into adulthood, city life became ingrained in her soul.

One day, in those years, she had met a man who was new in town.
Or at least she hadn't seen him before. Lot seemed a little different
but in a charming sort of way. She learned he had arrived recently
after moving away from his uncle Abraham's household. Soon Lot
was hanging out with her, enjoying all the perks that city life affords.

Not long after, they fell in love and were married. Soon two
daughters were born into their home. And Lot was becoming an influential member of the community. As the years passed, their daughters
grew and were betrothed to be married. Now their home was filled
with the excitement of two weddings. Sure, the city seemed to have
taken a downturn, but it was still home, so Lot's wife embraced it.

One evening, as her husband sat at the city gate, two strangers
arrived. As usual, her husband, being the eager host that he was, invited
them to stay in their home. The strangers hesitated, but her husband

insisted they not stay unprotected in the city. After some persuasion, the two strangers consented.

As night fell upon their home, evil men from the city pounded incessantly on the door. Lot tried in vain to appease the demands of this cruel crowd of men, even offering his daughters for their wicked designs. Turning on Lot, the mob pressed in with fierce determination, intent on breaking down the door. But the two strangers, angels sent from God, pulled Lot back inside his home, slammed the door shut, and struck the mob outside with blindness. Then the angels shocked Lot and his family with their dire pronouncement. "Get everyone out of here! God has sent us to destroy this place!"

Lot's wife, still shaken by the violent scene she had just witnessed, struggled to process the weight of the angels' devastating words. Leave? How could she leave? Her beloved city—destroyed? In a panic, she began to run through her home room by room. She grabbed her favorite silk cloak and her best woven linens. She filled her pockets with gold coins and her finest jewelry. Then, as the light of dawn broke over the horizon, the angels insisted the entire family leave immediately, lest they be swept away in the impending destruction.

Lot's wife hesitated. Seeing her uncertainty, an angel grabbed her by the hand and began dragging her out of the home despite her firm resistance. The gold coins fell from her pockets, scattering wildly across the hard floor. Her silk cloak slid off her shoulders and to the ground as the angel dragged her toward the street.

"Wait!" she cried, trying to retrieve her cloak while jewelry tumbled onto the street below.

But the angel, stronger than she was, continued to drag her through the dimly lit city until they were outside the gates. With a loud voice, he commanded them, "Flee for your lives! Don't look back! Do not stop anywhere!"

As the sun rose and their beloved city faded in the distance, the stench of burning sulfur filled her nostrils, and the smoke of destruction choked her until she could not breathe. In her heart, she knew it was all gone. Everything she had worked for, saved, and loved. The homes, the streets, the businesses—all gone. Even her friends. The angel's deafening cry of danger continued to echo in her ears. "Don't look back . . . don't look back."

But still, she wondered. Why was it so bad to look back? What could possibly be wrong with just one more glance at what she had loved and left behind? The air was so thick with smoke, no one would even see. So with one silent, measured turn of her head, and with a deliberate shift of her eyes, she took one last glance back—back to the glitter and glamour, back to the riches and intrigue of the sin-filled city she still loved more than anything. And in that fatal instant, as one last breath escaped her lips, she froze into a salty statue, her lifeless eyes now permanently fixed on the charred plains of destruction once known as Sodom and Gomorrah.

Unhindered faith in God comes when I am willing to let go of earthly things I love because I love God more.

Deepening Our Understanding

If your house was burning down, what would be the first things (besides family and pets) you would attempt to save? Why would you choose these?

_____

_____

_____

_____

_____

When Things Are Bad *(Read Genesis 19:1–11)*

From the beginning of this story, it is clear the situation in Sodom is not good. While sitting at the city gate, Lot meets two angels sent by God. He seems to know they are divine visitors, as he insists they come to his home rather than stay in the city where they will be at great risk. Later, when evil men from the city come knocking on Lot's door looking for the two angels, Lot betrays his daughters in a shocking way. But the two men sent from God rescue Lot and his family from this awful situation.

1. Do you think Lot knows how sinful the people of the city are? What elements of the story reveal this?

_____

_____

_____

_____

2. Has there been a time when you knew how bad things were, but you weren't ready to admit it? How did that situation turn out?

_____

_____

_____

_____

When Things Go from Bad to Worse *(Read Genesis 19:12–22)*
After a long, horrible night, the angels confront Lot and his family
with the news of God's pending destruction of their city, followed by
the command to leave immediately. But Lot's sons-in-law respond to
his pleading to flee with laughter, thinking Lot is joking. There is no
indication that these young men left Sodom before God's judgment fell.

3. Looking at the response of Lot's sons-in-law, what might you
    assume about the spiritual influence Lot has on his family?

_____

_____

_____

_____

_____

4. In a time of crisis for you or your family, do you have spiritual
    resources to draw on? Are you able to influence others to do
    the right thing in a tough situation?

_____

_____

_____

_____

_____

5. The first mention of Lot's wife is in these verses. She is not
    willing to leave their home on her own. The angel must take
    her by the hand and forcibly remove her. What might she
    be thinking as she is forced to leave?

_____

_____

_____

_____

_____

6. What makes you hold on to negative things in your life, even if you know God wants something better for you? What would make it easier to let these things go?

_____

_____

_____

_____

_____

When God's Judgment Is Thorough and Final (Read Genesis 19:23–26)

The first pleas to leave the city come from the angels to Lot and his family in the dark of night. At dawn the angels are still begging them to leave. Not until the sun has fully risen did Lot's family finally leave the city. Then the full wrath of God's judgment rains down on Sodom and Gomorrah, overthrowing "those cities and all the valley, and all the inhabitants of the cities, and what grew on the ground." Nothing is left after God's judgment is complete.

The second mention of Lot's wife occurs in verse 26. She cannot let go of what she has left behind. In that one devastating moment when she looks back, disobeying God's command, the life evaporates from her body as she becomes a pillar of salt.

7. What thoughts come to mind as you consider the decision of Lot's wife to look back? What would you say to her if you could meet her today?

_____

_____

_____

_____

_____

_____

8. Why do you think Lot's wife is never given her own name in the Bible? Perhaps she was named after what she loved most. What would your name be if you were named after what you loved most?

_____
_____
_____
_____
_____
_____

It is possible Lot's wife neither knew nor loved God. Perhaps Lot never told her about God. While God executes justice on evil, he also extends salvation to those who come to him by faith. There is hope in the mercy and grace of God!

9. Do you have a loved one who is walking down a path of destruction away from God, similar to the path Lot and his family were on? What does this story say to you?

_____
_____
_____
_____
_____
_____

Journal Page

Has God ever had to drag you kicking and screaming out of a bad situation because you wouldn't step away from it on your own? What did you learn from this situation?

_____

_____

_____

_____

_____

_____

Prayer Response

Do you desire to have a faith in God that is not held back by things of this world? What stands in your way? Write a prayer expressing your desire for a faith in God unhindered by things of this world. Perhaps include any steps you are willing to take to let go of these worldly cares.

_____

_____

_____

_____

_____

Nobody buys stock in a company that is sure to go bankrupt. Nobody sets up house in a sinking ship. No reasonable person would lay up treasure where moth and rust destroy and thieves break in and steal, would they? The world is passing away! To set your heart on it is only asking for heartache and misery in the end.

—John Piper[4]

4. John Piper, "Do Not Love the World," *Sermons*. March 10, 1985. *Desiring God.* https://www.desiringgod.org/messages/do-not-love-the-world.

CHAPTER 6

Letting Go of Rejection

ANGER. SHAME. SADNESS. ANXIETY. PAINFUL EMOTIONS TUMBLE OVER themselves every time those memories of rejection flood your mind. What did you do to deserve being left out, considered unwanted, treated as worthless? What if the pain never goes away?

Trusting in the Desert

It had all happened so fast in some ways. It seemed like just yesterday she had been cradling her newborn son in her arms. But here she was, huddled near the ground and weak with exhaustion, watching her son, now a young man, struggle as the pangs of death shuddered through his body. Her agonizing terror of losing him was interrupted by momentary flashes of anger over the injustice that had brought them to this point. What had she ever done to deserve this?

Hagar had long ago given up being granted any more than what life had handed her. She knew that in the eyes of other people, she did not deserve any more than she had been given. She had started off as a servant, or as some preferred to call her, a handmaid. Her wealthy owners, Abram and Sarai, had sufficiently provided her with her basic needs. And they had called upon her to assist them personally, in contrast to the servants who worked in the fields or prepared food for the large group of people in their charge. So she kept silent and did her job well, knowing it probably would not get much better than this.

Then there was that one surprising, heart-wrenching request— one she could not believe had been asked of her. But indeed, it was. Infertility was a curse no woman wanted to face, including her master's wife. So Hagar was charged with the responsibility of bearing Abram a child—an heir—as was customary for this situation. Her mistress, Sarai, made all the arrangements to carry out this plan. Suddenly, she was no longer a servant. She was the wife of one of the most famous and wealthiest patriarchs of the region, bearing for him his first child—the heir to his inheritance. What a turn of events! She relished her new position and loved her new son. Finally, she mattered. She was a person of worth. Or so she thought.

Eventually her mistress also bore a son to Abram, naming him Isaac. This son was considered their child of promise—a gift from God. In Sarai's eyes, Hagar and her teenage son, Ishmael, became despised, viewed as mere slaves who had no place in Abram's household. One day, when Hagar could no longer take the abuse, she and Ishmael left, having been given some provisions by Abram, who had always treated them with compassion.

Hagar headed south toward Egypt, thinking she could make it all the way home. But the desert roads proved too difficult. In desperation, she stopped to rest. She recalled meeting the One she came to know as "the God who sees"—the One who found her alone in the desert sixteen years before when she had fled as a young pregnant woman from Sarai's mistreatment. This was the One who had given her the name for her son—Ishmael. How she loved to say his name and its meaning! "Ishmael," she whispered again. "The God who hears." Sixteen years ago, in obedience to this God she had come to know, she had returned to her master's household and raised her son there.

The groans of her dying son pierced her heart. Once again, she had left her mistress, fleeing to a desert place. Once again, she had no more resources, no more hope. *The God who sees—where is he now?* Sobs shook her body until she could barely breathe.

Suddenly, Hagar's sobs were interrupted by a voice she had heard before. Yes, she knew this voice! The God who hears was speaking to her, telling her to not be afraid—her son would live. The God who sees was opening her eyes to see a well nearby, providing lifesaving water for her son. In that moment, her despair turned to hope, her disbelief turned to trust. Despite the most difficult of circumstances, she could trust her God—the God who sees and hears.

Unhindered faith in God comes when I choose to listen to his Word and look for his work in my most difficult circumstances.

Deepening Our Understanding

What circumstances have caused you to feel isolated or alone? How do you cope when this happens?

_____

_____

_____

_____

_____

_____

A First Encounter with God in the Wilderness *(Read Genesis 16:1–7)*

Hagar, pregnant with Abram's child, becomes the object of scorn and mistreatment from Abram's wife, Sarai. In desperation, Hagar flees into the wilderness, alone and abandoned by all who have cared for her. Yet she is not alone. The angel of the Lord finds her by a spring of water and speaks to her.

1. The word *find* suggests that God is looking for Hagar. What does this tell you about his relationship to Hagar at this time? Do you think Hagar expects to find God in the wilderness?

_____

_____

_____

_____

_____

2. How would you describe your relationship with God right now? Has God found you in any wilderness times you've encountered?

_____

_____

_____

_____

_____

A Conversation with God in the Wilderness *(Read Genesis 16:8–13)*

The angel of the Lord asks Hagar two questions: Where has she come from? Where is she going? Hagar answers only one question with information about where she has come from.

3. Why do you think Hagar neglects to answer God's question about where she is going?

    _____

    _____

    _____

    _____

4. If God asked you these questions—where have you come from and where are you going—how would you answer based on your current situation?

    _____

    _____

    _____

    _____

A Second Encounter with God in the Wilderness *(Read Genesis 21:8–21)*

God orchestrates a second encounter with Hagar sixteen years later in a place similar to the first encounter—and for similar reasons. Only this time, Hagar is distraught as her son nears death because of their lack of food and water. Hagar, unable to watch him suffer, positions herself a short distance away as agonizing cries of grief wrack her body.

5. Do you think Hagar is hoping God will meet her in the wilderness again?

    _____

    _____

    _____

    _____

6. If you are facing a difficult time right now, what memories of God's past work come to your mind? Do you believe God can do this again for you?

_____

_____

_____

_____

_____

_____

Journal Response

In Hagar's first encounter with God, she is traveling on the road to Shur. In her second encounter, she is in the wilderness of Beersheba. In both situations, she appears to be headed in the direction of Egypt, perhaps going back to her home. When situations get difficult, where do you tend to want to go back to? Where do you think you should go instead?

_____

_____

_____

_____

_____

Prayer Response

Hagar's first encounter with God gives her the courage to acknowledge her new relationship with him in a unique way—she gives him a name. She calls him *El Roi*, the God who sees.

If you could give God a name based on your experience of walking with him during the hard times, what name would you choose? Write a prayer to God, using the name you chose. Your prayer can be either a prayer of request for God's help in a current troublesome circumstance or a prayer of thanks for God's help in a past situation.

_____

_____

_____

_____

When we are tired of trying to be good enough and together enough, when we are tired of juggling the complexities and fighting against the tides of confusion, when we are ready to stop striving and receive the gift . . . Jesus is there.

—Claire Cloninger[5]

---

5. Claire Cloninger, *A Place Called Simplicity* (Eugene, OR: Harvest House Publishers, 1993), 180.

PART 4

Giving God Access to My Tough Stuff

The Back Room

THE NEW FARMHOUSE WAS BUILT THE SUMMER AFTER THE FIRE. MY DAD, a mechanical engineer by trade, had also built the house we were living in. So he and my mom, along with help from others, decided to build a new house for my grandparents. That summer after school was out, my sister and I spent many days exploring and playing at the farm while my dad built the new house.

Because my grandparents were growing older, my dad designed this home to accommodate their needs. We watched as the house took shape: a modern kitchen, spacious living room, and three bedrooms, all in a one-floor ranch. By early fall, my grandparents had settled in and were enjoying their new home.

In this house, my grandma had what we affectionately called the back room. It was the bedroom directly at the end of the hall. Grandma stored everything in this back room. Books. Blankets. Shoes. Greeting cards. Gifts from the previous Christmas that she didn't use but kept because she loved the ones who gave them to her. An old phone that had long since been replaced. And more. These items ended up in the back room because she didn't know what to do with them but couldn't get rid of them.

The back room fascinated my sister and me as young girls. Often we would spend an entire day at my grandparents' home while my mom helped Grandma clean her house or catch up on her mail. My sister and I usually began the day by visiting the cows in the barn or helping Grandpa with a few easy farm chores. After Grandma heated up frozen pizza for a quick lunch, it was time for us to explore that room down the hall and create our own imaginary adventure with the collection of interesting items found there.

In later years, we would offer to help Grandma organize the back room. But usually, she told us not to bother. We loved her, and we understood. She wasn't ready to deal with the work involved and the decisions she would have to make to clean it out. That would have to wait for another day.

Like my grandma, sometimes we have emotional things we don't want to deal with, so we stuff them into the back room of our hearts. We know what the issues are, but we aren't ready to do the work involved or make the decisions we need to make. But the issues we have hidden in the back room of our hearts hinder our ability to exercise faith in God.

Faith unhindered becomes my experience when I unpack the back room of my heart and deal with the issues I have hidden there, giving them back to God.

CHAPTER 7

Letting Go of Criticism

IT STARTS OFF AS JUST A LITTLE COMPLAINT. NOTHING SERIOUS. MAYBE a bit of bad attitude. But you have it under control, safely tucked away in that secret back room of your heart. No one will know. But then a little disrespect slips out. Then more disrespect. Soon cynicism is slipping through the cracks. Pride is pushing away your common sense. But you still have it under control. Or so you think.

Pursuing Humility

Her brother's decision didn't make sense. Why would he marry that woman? Not that there was anything particularly wrong with her. It's just that, well—she was different. She didn't come from the same people, the same background, the same history that Miriam held so dear. And on top of the disappointing news of Moses's marriage, Miriam was bugged that he hadn't even asked for her opinion on his decision. After all, she was the older sister—shouldn't she have been consulted?

Allowing her mind to wander back to other times Moses had gotten on her nerves, Miriam's irritation increased. What about that time when he appointed seventy elders to help him manage the needs of their people? He hadn't consulted her about that decision either. And the miracle God did when they all crossed the Red Sea on dry ground? Moses ended up in the spotlight again, as he always did. He probably had forgotten she was the reason he was even here. If their mother had not sent her to watch over her baby brother in that basket on the river, who knows what would have happened to him?

To make matters worse, her brother seemed oblivious to the incredible influence he had as their leader. A spirit of genuine humility marked everything he did. In fact, it was downright annoying. Why did he have to be so humble? It made her tendency to be bossy look worse than it really was.

It was time, she decided. Enough of being the second-place sister. Enough of being overlooked when important decisions were made. Who had decided, anyway, that God only spoke through Moses? It was time for her voice to be heard too.

Noticing her other brother, Aaron, nearby, Miriam decided to find out his opinion about Moses's marriage. But she already knew Aaron would go along with her—he always did. After all, he got along with everyone and didn't make waves. Leaning toward him, she whispered in his ear, "Don't you think Moses should have married someone else? I mean, what was he thinking?" Aaron nodded in agreement, much to her delight. She continued, the irritation in her voice increasing. "Don't you think the Lord speaks through us also—not just through Moses?"

At that moment, without warning, the voice of God thundered across the sky. He called out Miriam's name, along with her two brothers, telling them to go to his meeting place, for he had something to say to them. Miriam's mind raced. She thought her conversation had been a private one between her and Aaron. Had God been listening in? Did God see the critical spirit within her? Miriam's face grew pale as she considered the seriousness of what she had just done.

With every step toward the Tent of Meeting, Miriam's heart pounded with dread. She covered her eyes as the pillar of cloud descended on the tent. God had arrived. And he wanted to talk to her. She felt slightly relieved when God called Aaron to step forward with her. Maybe she wouldn't be singled out after all. Aaron had gone along with it, too, so it was only right that he would also be judged.

"Hear my words," God commanded, his voice thundering through the Tent of Meeting. "My servant Moses is not like you nor like anyone else. With him I speak clearly. He looks upon my form. You do not. Why are you not afraid to speak against him?" And with that, God departed, leaving them standing there in silence.

Miriam didn't move, her shaking knees making her momentarily unstable. Her brothers stood in stunned silence beside her. Turning to look at her, their eyes widened. Confused, she looked down at her hands and feet. A muffled scream escaped her lips. Diseased skin covered her entire body. Leprosy!

How could this be? Just seconds before, she had been in perfect health. Now she had a contagious disease with no cure. Just seconds before, she was a well-respected woman among her people. Now she would be banished outside the camp for the rest of her life, watching people she loved from a distance, calling out "Unclean! Unclean!" anytime someone accidentally came too close. She cried out in her spirit, *No, God! Please, no!* But God did not answer.

Turning to her brothers, she looked at them with pleading eyes, unable to put into words the agony in her soul. And it was Moses, her humble brother, the one she had so sharply criticized, who cried out to God on her behalf with a simple prayer: "O God, please heal her."

The voice of God spoke to Moses. Seven days outside the camp. Then Miriam could return. She would be healed. Tears of relief fell as Miriam wrapped her garment tightly around her now-diseased body. As she prepared herself for the days ahead—the shame, the pain, the isolation—she was still thankful for a God who could heal, who could forgive her sin, and who had heard and answered the prayer of her amazing brother.

Unhindered faith thrives when I seek a spirit of humility
and guard against a spirit of criticism.

Deepening Our Understanding

Has there ever been a time when you turned a small problem into a major problem with your words? What happened in this situation? Were you able to fix it?

_____

_____

_____

_____

_____

Turning a Minor Situation into a Major Conflict *(Read Numbers 12:1–2)*

The Bible gives no preliminary information about this incident in Miriam's life. The reader is brought into the story with Miriam and Aaron already talking about their disagreement with their brother Moses's marriage. The conversation moves quickly from a complaint about a family matter to a larger complaint about a leadership matter. But they have forgotten one important truth: God hears every word they speak.

1. What is the larger complaint that Miriam and Aaron have, which becomes evident at the end of this conversation? Based on this larger complaint, how would you describe what Miriam's criticism is really about?

_____

_____

_____

_____

2. In what situation have you tried to disguise your real criticism under the guise of a lesser issue? How did that go?

_____

_____

_____

_____

Getting the Facts Straight *(Read Numbers 12:3–9)*
Miriam and Aaron, while focused on what they think isn't right about the situation, have either neglected to remember or are not aware of the dynamic relationship that exists between Moses and God. God does not hesitate to remind them of this, providing specific details regarding how Moses is able to behold God and how he and God speak to one another. God makes it clear that his relationship with Moses is unique. Miriam and Aaron were wrong to go down the path of comparison and assume that God relates to each of them in the same manner. This conversation ends abruptly when God departs, his anger kindled against Miriam and Aaron.

3. Miriam and Aaron get caught in the trap of comparing themselves with their brother in a manner that elevates themselves. How is the trap of comparison closely related to criticism? What should Miriam have done to keep herself from being ensnared?

_____

_____

_____

_____

_____

_____

4. Do you know someone who seems to have a closer relationship with God than you do? If so, how does that make you feel? Do you find yourself ensnared in the trap of comparison, which sometimes leads you toward a spirit of criticism? Are you more likely to criticize yourself or others?

_____

_____

_____

_____

_____

_____

Understanding the Dangers *(Read Numbers 12:10–12)*

In this time, leprosy, a very contagious disease, is feared by all. The disease spreads rapidly if not dealt with using extreme measures. Immediate isolation is essential for control. With no treatment or cure available at this point, leprosy is also fatal. Aaron describes a leper as "one dead, whose flesh is half eaten away" (v. 12). The prognosis Miriam faces as a leper is devastating.

Like leprosy, criticism carries with it a concern and consequence. If left unchecked, a spirit of criticism quickly spreads, moving rapidly from person to person until it turns into a public wave of criticism, affecting many people and sweeping out of control. Criticism can also bring disastrous consequences, first for the individual who spreads it and ultimately for all those who contract the spirit of criticism from that individual.

Miriam's criticism of Moses's leadership was just as dangerous to God's people as Miriam's leprosy would have been. God made her a visible example of this lesson to teach her and to teach all of us about the serious effects of a critical spirit.

5. What symptoms (warning signs) might Miriam have missed that would have revealed the critical spirit taking hold of her?

_____

_____

_____

_____

_____

6. What might be warning signs in your own life that a spirit of criticism is taking hold of you?

_____

_____

_____

_____

_____

_____

Discovering the Solution: Prayer *(Read Numbers 12:13–16)*
Moses and Aaron are just as distraught as Miriam when they recognize her leprous condition. While Aaron speaks on behalf of his sister, Moses is the one who calls out to God for Miriam's healing—a simple prayer and the only words Moses speaks in this entire encounter. God answers Moses's prayer by limiting the duration of Miriam's disease to seven days.

7. Throughout this story, it is evident God is displeased with Miriam's actions. Even though Aaron goes along with her judgment of Moses, God singles out Miriam for the punishment of leprosy. What does this tell you about how God views a spirit of criticism?

_____

_____

_____

_____

_____

8. Moses only talks to one person throughout this entire incident—God. He asks God to heal his sister, the one who has been most critical of him. What can you learn from the example of Moses regarding how to respond to criticism from others?

_____

_____

_____

_____

9. Why is it hard to be a person of criticism and a person of prayer at the same time?

_____

_____

_____

_____

Journal Response

What are you currently dealing with that causes you to have a critical spirit? What are the consequences of your critical spirit? How might you be able to replace this with a spirit of humility instead?

_____

_____

_____

_____

_____

Prayer Response

God and Moses had a close relationship. How would you describe your current relationship with God? Is it close? Or distant? If you feel close to God, perhaps you can express your thankfulness to him. If you feel distant from God, how would you express your desire to have a closer relationship with him?

_____

_____

_____

_____

_____

> We can start to expect a lot—from life, from work, from others in general—until no matter what we're receiving in terms of blessing, it's never as much as we were hoping for. Needing God but not always wanting God, we expect others to take the place of God in our lives, depending on them to guide our decisions, to love us continuously and unconditionally, to provide for us emotionally, physically, socially, totally. And when they disappoint us—which inevitably happens—rather than being grateful for God's unchanging love and His faithfulness in meeting our needs, those unfulfilled expectations easily turn into resentment that poisons our hearts and relationships.
>
> —Nancy Leigh Demoss Wolgemuth[6]

---

6. Nancy Leigh DeMoss Wolgemuth, *Choosing Gratitude: Your Journey to Joy* (Chicago, IL: Moody Publishers, 2009), 53.

CHAPTER 8

Letting Go of Bitterness

IT JUST ISN'T FAIR. WHAT DID YOU DO TO DESERVE THIS? YOU'VE
worked harder than most to do life right. You're there for your family
when they need something. You support your friends in their tough
times. Why can't something go right for you—just once? Sometimes
it seems like the whole world is against you. Maybe even God.

Choosing to Trust God

She watched her husband sitting in the corner of the room, speechless
in his misery. As if the grief were not enough, now his own illness had
left him weak and miserable. Without lifting his eyes to acknowledge
her, Job silently picked the scabs off the pus-filled blisters cover-
ing his body.

Waves of grief had been drowning the voice in her own soul for
weeks. At times she could hardly get out of bed, the weight of sorrow
leaving her feeling breathless as soon as she opened her eyes in the
morning. Other days she simply moved around the house, oblivious
to her surroundings. There were no words to be spoken, nothing to
talk about—not while images of the fresh graves of her ten children
still flooded her mind.

But today—this one horribly miserable day—her grief suddenly
disappeared in an undertow beneath massive waves of anger. Her heart
raced and tears burned in her eyes as she stared at the collection of
sandals still piled by the door and the empty chairs around the table
where her children once enjoyed meals. Then she broke the silence
with four awful words: "Curse God and die!"

Her voice shattered the endless silence that had engulfed the space, spewing bitterness across the room straight to the heart of her suffering husband. Those words, that voice—it didn't even sound like her own. Had she really said that? Job lifted his dark, hollow eyes and looked straight at her without saying a word. She knew what his look meant. Yes, she had indeed spoken those miserable words—words that reflected the thoughts that had tormented her for days. *Curse God and die! Let's just put an end to this misery. It's not worth it!*

She waited for Job to respond. After a prolonged moment of painful silence, Job implored her. "Please don't talk like other women who are foolish," he said. "That's not who you are. I know you better than that. Remember the good God did for us before all this happened? We loved God then, didn't we? How can we be so eager to accept God's good gifts then but reject him now when he allows hardship? He is still the same God who loves us."

She remained silent. Her husband's words rang with a hollow echo in her heart. Perhaps Job was right. Perhaps God was indeed good. But for now, her final words remained just that—final.

Unhindered faith comes when I choose to trust God in the midst of grief, believing he is my source of hope and confidence for the future.

Deepening Our Understanding

What experience has left you feeling the most vulnerable—the least in control of your circumstances? What did you do to get through this challenging time?

_____

_____

_____

_____

_____

A Surprising Question *(Read Job 2:1–9a)*

Are you still holding on to your integrity? This is the only question the Bible records Job's wife asking. After suffering the tragic deaths of all their children in addition to the loss of most of their livelihood, Job and his wife struggle to move on. They struggle to get out of bed in the morning. They struggle to even talk to each other. Job's wife knows her husband is a man of integrity. In fact, everyone knows that, including Satan. For most of their lives, it seems, Job's character has brought him respect and honor in his home and community. But Job's integrity hasn't proven worthwhile in this situation. It hasn't protected them from this disaster. And Job's integrity doesn't permit him to strike back in anger at the God who has allowed this tragedy. So what good has integrity done for them?

We often assume that God blesses the righteous and judges the wicked. Job's story begins with a conversation between God and Satan based on this premise: Job has served God only because God has blessed him. Satan suggests that if everything is taken away from Job, he will not serve God. Surprisingly, God permits Satan to do this, limiting only his power to take Job's life. Thus, we find Job and his wife thrust into the most unimaginable tragedy possible.

1. Do you think it is possible that Job's wife has begun to believe that a good woman deserves a good life? How might this thinking affect her understanding of God in the midst of this tragedy?

_____

_____

_____

_____

2. Do you believe that a good woman deserves a good life? Has there been a time in your life when doing the right thing didn't seem to pay off in the end? How might this thinking affect your understanding of God in hard times?

_____

_____

_____

_____

A Shocking Statement *(Read Job 2:9b)*

Curse God and die. This is the only statement the Bible records Job's wife making. Her life is so miserable at this point, there seems to be nothing left to live for—not even God. But take a moment to think of all the other words she has spoken in her lifetime. Words of joy at the birth of each of her ten children. Words of instruction as she has managed a large household. Words of encouragement to her husband as he has risen in prominence in their community. Now it seems the only words people will remember from her are words of bitterness and blame.

3. As you think of all the life experiences Job's wife has enjoyed, what are some words you can imagine her speaking to her husband, her children, her friends?

_____

_____

_____

_____

4. What do you want people to remember about what you say?

_____

_____

_____

_____

_____

A Sobering Reply (Read Job 2:10)

You speak as a foolish woman. These are Job's words in response to his wife's brutal statement. No doubt he knows she is buried under the same weight of grief he is. But he also knows where her thinking will lead—to a pit of doubt and despair she may never come out of.

Then Job asks his wife a question—but it is really a question for us all: Will we only accept the good things from God but not the bad things? Not the hard things? Is that all we want God in our lives for—to make our journey through this life pleasant and easy? It is a sobering question to consider.

Sometimes, even after all the good things God has done, we lose faith when disaster strikes. We allow ourselves to think that God either doesn't know or he doesn't care. When we start to expect only good things from God and not hard things, we end up in a place of bitterness toward him for allowing the hard and horrible things we encounter. Job knows that. He does not want to end up in that place of bitterness and doubt. And he doesn't want his wife to go there either.

5. If you could read a page in the journal of Job's wife after she has this conversation with her husband, what do you think she might have written about God? About her husband? About herself?

_____

_____

_____

_____

_____

6. Have you ever found yourself in a pit of doubt and despair after a time of severe trial? Did you allow yourself to think that God didn't know or didn't care? What enabled you to get out of that pit of doubt and choose to trust God?

_____

_____

_____

_____

_____

A Surprising Restoration *(Read Job 42:10–17)*

God restores all that has been taken from Job and his wife—in some cases even more abundantly.

When they are in the middle of their severe trial, Job and his wife do not know that God will later restore everything they have lost and more. Yet Job does not give up on his faith in God. He holds firm to what he believes to be true about God's character and his plan for them. And God proves himself faithful again.

While no mention of Job's wife is specifically given at the conclusion of Job's story, it is probable that Job's wife remains with him throughout their lifetimes. Thus, she also receives God's blessing of seven more sons and three more daughters, along with the physical properties and resources that God restores to them. Job's story concludes with the blessing of enjoying four generations of his family after coming through this time of trial as a man of integrity.

7. Have you ever experienced restoration after a trial or loss? Or have you observed restoration happen for a friend? What does this story of restoration tell you about God?

_____

_____

_____

_____

8. What story of restoration are you waiting for? What do you
    hope God will do or change? What helps you hold onto faith
    in God while you wait?

_____

_____

_____

_____

_____

_____

Journal Response

Has there been a time of trial when you found it difficult to believe
God would come through for you? Do you find yourself in that place
now? Do you need to let go of any bitterness or lack of faith in God?

_____

_____

_____

_____

_____

Prayer Response

What have you learned from Job and his wife that can enable you to trust God in difficulty? Are you ready to place your faith in God completely for your salvation? For your past, your future, your fears, and your hurts? God wants you to find the freedom to trust him completely. Are you ready to do that today?

_____

_____

_____

_____

_____

> *We have to decide if we will let go of our control over a person, situation or event, or if we will hang on for dear life and refuse to relinquish something we cherish . . . . Will we maintain our grip on hope in the process of defeat? Will we live our lives with passion and purpose, even if, in this lifetime, we are not permitted to have an answer to why something has happened? Will we choose unshakable faith, or will we give up on God? I believe God's greatest invitation is to engage us in the process of discovering the power of choosing faith when that decision makes no sense.*
>
> —Carol Kent[7]

---

7. Carol Kent, *When I Lay My Isaac Down* (Colorado Springs, CO: NavPress, 2004), 12–13.

ORDER INFORMATION

CPSIA information can be obtained
at www.ICGtesting.com
Printed in the USA
BVHW081953090222
627929BV00004B/11